THE LOUDEST SCREEN KISS
and other little-known facts
about the movies

The Loudest Screen Kiss

and other little-known facts about the movies

Written and Illustrated by Barbara Seuling

Doubleday & Company, Inc., Garden City, New York

LIBRARY OF CONGRESS CATALOG CARD NUMBER 76–2824
ISBN 0-385-11424-9 TRADE
0-385-11425-7 PREBOUND
COPYRIGHT © 1976 BY BARBARA SEULING
ALL RIGHTS RESERVED
PRINTED IN THE UNITED STATES OF AMERICA
FIRST EDITION

For Tom, affectionately

*Many thanks to Dennis Seuling
and Mickey Tennenbaum,
who shared their knowledge,
enthusiasm, and good humor with me
during the course of this book,
and to the Lincoln Center Library
of the Performing Arts.*

THE LOUDEST SCREEN KISS
and other little-known facts
about the movies

Lucille Ball was once dismissed from a drama school for being "too shy and reticent."

The gigantic monster in *The Beast from 20,000 Fathoms* was actually a model about two feet high, filmed against miniature backgrounds.

Clark Gable failed his first screen tests because his ears were too big.

When Jean Harlow died suddenly in 1937, her last picture, *Saratoga*, remained unfinished. The studio completed it using her double, Mary Dees.

Lou Costello, of the comedy team Abbott and Costello, was once a prizefighter.

In the silent film *What Price Glory?*, lip readers in the audience discovered that the players had had a field day cursing and swearing.

The first dog to become a film star was "Strongheart."

Robert Redford's nose has been broken five times.

At the second wedding of Elizabeth Taylor and Richard Burton, two of the spectators were hippopotami.

In a sequel to *The Mummy*, a stunt man who doubled for a star was wrapped head to toe in linen bandages. All day long there were delays, to spray paint the bandages to look tattered, to wait for the paint to dry, for the rest of the crew to have lunch, and through many retakes. For the entire time, the stunt man could not move to stretch, eat, or go to the bathroom. By the end of the day, on the verge of insanity, he was quickly torn out of his costume and revived, but has since had a fear of being closed in in small places.

In 1939, fifty million people went to the movies.

The longest kiss in films occurs in Alfred Hitchcock's *Notorious* between Cary Grant and Ingrid Bergman.

Marge Champion, who later was half of the Marge and Gower Champion dance team, was the physical model for Snow White in Walt Disney's *Snow White and the Seven Dwarfs,* and for the Blue Fairy in *Pinocchio.*

An RKO picture in 1933 could not have the word "filthy" in it.

Charlie Chaplin made thirty-five films in 1914.

In 1928, the first and only Academy Award was presented for the best title writing. Until 1927, movies were silent and the action was explained on titles shown beneath the pictures. By the next year, sound films had replaced silents, and that category was no longer necessary.

The world's widest movie screen was first exhibited at the Paris Exposition in 1900. It was a circular wall on which were projected ten separate films, making up one gigantic film all around. The audience was in the center.

The picture on which the most stunt men were killed—three—was the 1930 film *Hell's Angels*. In the same year, the worst incident during the production of a film took place. Two planes, on their way to shoot a scene in *Such Men Are Dangerous,* collided in mid-air over the Pacific, killing ten members of the film crew.

All of the arrows in the picture *The Adventures of Robin Hood* with Errol Flynn were shot by Howard Hill, the most famous archer in the world, including one in which one arrow splits another already in the bull's-eye. (In the picture it looks as if this arrow is shot by Robin Hood.)

When actor Bela Lugosi died, he was buried in his Dracula cloak.

From 1924 to 1974, M-G-M produced 1,705 movies.

Fredric March was the only actor ever to receive an Academy Award for a role in a horror film, for *Dr. Jekyll and Mr. Hyde.*

The photoplay Gold Medal Award, the oldest award in the film industry, has been given more often to Bing Crosby than to any other movie star . . . five times.

For Cecil B. DeMille's 1929 sound film *Dynamite,* the theme song was "Dynamite, Dynamite, Blow Back My Sweetie to Me."

Bob Hope was once a boxer. He used the name Packy East.

When *Frankenstein* and *Dracula* were first released, nurses and ambulances were in attendance at the movie theaters.

The director of *Jaws,* Steven Spielberg, was only twenty-six years old when he worked on the film.

Leslie Caron and Tab Hunter were born on exactly the same day: July 1, 1931.

Movie theater personnel were once so thoroughly trained that ushers who escorted patrons to their seats could only refer to a man as "gentleman" and a woman as "madam" and, if asked his opinion of a picture, had to reply, "The comments are very favorable. I am sure you will enjoy it."

It is estimated that during the shooting of *The Good Humor Man,* starring Jack Carson, six thousand pies were thrown in one week on the sound stage.

The shower scene in *Psycho,* which has become famous, was composed of seventy different camera shots shown in forty-five seconds on the screen. None of the torso shots was of Janet Leigh.

Myra Franklin of Cardiff, Wales, sat through *The Sound of Music* 940 times.

The only picture actor Charles Laughton ever directed was *Night of the Hunter* with Robert Mitchum and Shelley Winters.

Marlene Dietrich entertained the troops in USO shows during World War II by playing the musical saw.

In the early days of movies, some theaters had live actors behind the screen to speak the lines of the actors. In Thailand today, some theaters still use this method.

In 1929, it cost about thirty-five cents to go to the movies.

The famous ballet at the end of *An American in Paris* might never have been in the picture had it not been for Nina Foch's chicken pox. At that point the plot had been resolved and there was some doubt as to whether to stick a ballet on the end at all; some thought it would be pointless and dull. But while they waited for Ms. Foch to recuperate, Gene Kelly and director Vincente Minnelli finished preparations and filmed the ballet.

For the special effects in *The Towering Inferno*, a huge building model was constructed, five stories tall. The building in the film was supposed to be about 130 stories high, which means the model had to squeeze about twenty-six stories into one. The model was built in a huge pit dug out of the ground on one of Twentieth Century-Fox's largest sound stages.

In 1936 there were 20,000 extras (people who were hired for crowd or background scenes) living in Hollywood.

The "B." in Cecil B. De Mille's name stands for "Blount."

The "O." in David O. Selznick's name stands for nothing. . . . He just thought it sounded more dignified than plain David Selznick.

In *The Poseidon Adventure*, Shelley Winters did her own swimming, instead of using a stunt woman or a double.

The first movie studio in Hollywood, established in 1911, was the Nestor Film Company, in an ex-tavern on the corner of Sunset Boulevard and Gower Street.

Rudolph Valentino's death at the age of thirty-one created hysteria throughout the country, with many women trying to commit suicide. At his funeral, hundreds of thousands of fans crowded to pay their last respects.

Fred Astaire's legs have been insured for a million dollars.

In 1915, when Universal opened its first studio, it included a productive chicken ranch on the grounds to help defray the cost of making movies.

Rock Hudson was once a postman.

Joan Blondell's given name was "Rosebud." Her sister's given name was "Lover."

The 1932 film *I Am a Fugitive from a Chain Gang,* starring Paul Muni, helped bring about humane changes in Georgia's penal system, where the chain gang was once common.

When M-G-M gave thirteen-year-old Judy Garland a contract, she was the only person in the history of that studio who was signed up without a screen or sound test.

In the chariot race scene in the 1959 version of *Ben Hur,* a chariot comes around the ring and in its way is the wreckage of another chariot which has not been cleared away. The driver jumps, with the chariot, over the wreckage, falls forward out of the chariot, and pulls himself back in. This spectacular stunt was pure accident, but the cameras were rolling and caught it on film, and it appeared in the final picture.

Rudolph Valentino was so popular that any actor with a Latin look or name became a hot property. The real name of Ricardo Cortez, who rode on this wave of popularity, was Jacob Stein.

The Soviet film *War and Peace* included a re-created battle scene which involved twelve thousand men and eight hundred horses.

In 1958 the Los Angeles Pet Cemetery held the remains of approximately twenty thousand movie animals and movie stars' pets.

Ann Miller, famous tap-dancing movie star, had rickets as a child and took ballet and acrobatic lessons to overcome it.

Some early screen actresses adopted film names that represented the types they wished to play: Bessie Love, Blanche Sweet, Louise Lovely, and Arline Pretty were some.

In 1883, Mr. and Mrs. Deida Wilcox of Topeka, Kansas, moved to some farmland in California, bought for $1.25 an acre, where they intended to raise figs. Mrs. Wilcox named it Hollywood in honor of two pots of English holly she had brought with her. The holly didn't last, but Hollywood did.

Lilli Palmer was born on a train between Vienna and Berlin.

The first animated cartoon, made in 1909, was *Gertie the Dinosaur*, created by Winsor McCay. It was drawn so that Gertie (in the film) would respond when McCay (on the stage) talked to her, and the two became quite a successful vaudeville act.

Betty Grable's legs were once insured for $1,250,000.

Roughly one quarter to one third of a movie audience's money goes for refreshments.

For the filming of a car chase scene in *The French Connection,* an area of Bensonhurst, in Brooklyn, was roped off, but a truck got through the barrier and hit a car which came speeding through. The studio got it on film, paid off the people for damages, and left the scene in the film.

Over the years, Radio City Music Hall in New York City has shown more of Cary Grant's films than any other actor's. Totaled up, his name has appeared on the marquee for fifteen months.

James Arness, who became known for his portrayal of Matt Dillon in TV's *Gunsmoke,* started his career in the movies, playing a frozen monster that came to life when thawed, in *The Thing.* He couldn't be seen (he was heavily costumed) or heard (he had no lines) throughout the picture.

On the set of *The Goldwyn Follies* in 1937, Edgar Bergen, the ventriloquist, and his dummy, Charlie McCarthy, were doing a scene. No matter how hard he tried, the sound man couldn't get the sound right. It turned out that whenever Charlie started to "speak," he turned the mike away from Bergen and toward the dummy.

John Wayne is the most successful star in screen history, according to box office statistics. His career in movies spans more than forty years, and includes some of the most famous Westerns ever made.

There were actually five Marx Brothers: Groucho, Chico, Harpo, Zeppo, and Gummo. Zeppo played straight roles rather than comedy, and Gummo never appeared in pictures. He opened a Hollywood talent agency instead.

Actor Herbert Marshall kept the fact that he had a wooden leg well concealed. Once, when Marlene Dietrich had a broken leg and wanted to get back to work quickly, she took lessons from Marshall on how to walk without a limp.

Dean Martin's real name is Dino Crocetti.

The first song to win an Academy Award was "The Continental," from the 1934 Fred Astaire/Ginger Rogers musical *The Gay Divorcee*.

Gene Autry, the singing cowboy who never resorted to violence in his Westerns, invested his money wisely and is today one of America's wealthiest men.

Theda Bara, the first screen "vamp," derived her film name from mixing up the letters in the words *Arab Death*.

Steve McQueen is a racing car driver in private life and does most of his own stunt driving in his pictures.

Alfred Hitchcock has a habit of appearing, very briefly, in each of his films. The most difficult to get in was his film *Lifeboat*, which takes place entirely in a small life raft adrift on the sea, with a few very defined characters. Hitchcock, nevertheless, managed to appear. Someone picks up a newspaper from the bottom of the boat, and on the back page an ad for a weight-reducing aid can be seen. Hitchcock is the "before" in "before" and "after" pictures in the ad.

Walter Huston, the actor, was the father of John Huston, the director.

A single frame of 35 mm film, when projected on the screen, is magnified from 50,000 to 300,000 times.

In their heyday, Louella Parsons and Hedda Hopper, the joint royalty of Hollywood gossip columnists, had a combined readership of seventy-five million people.

The lion that appears at the beginning of each M-G-M picture is named Jackie II.

John Wayne cooks his wife's favorite dishes for himself and members of his crew when they are away on location.

In the 1930s, Mickey Mouse had become so famous that he was given a place in the *Encyclopaedia Britannica.*

The only director to have received six Academy Awards is John Ford.

In the original *Frankenstein*, starring Boris Karloff, Karloff is given no screen credit. The monster was left a mystery, with a big question mark appearing on the screen in place of the actor's name.

Liza Minnelli, daughter of film star Judy Garland and film director Vincente Minnelli, made her screen debut at the age of 2½ as Judy Garland and Van Johnson's daughter in *The Good Old Summertime*.

Movie star Mickey Rooney's real name is Joe Yule, Jr.

Yakima Canutt, king of the Hollywood stunt men, did most of the spectacular staging of the chariot race in the 1959 version of *Ben Hur*. Canutt, who trained his own troupe of stunt men, was the favorite of William S. Hart, Tom Mix, Roy Rogers, John Wayne, and Clark Gable.

When M-G-M produced a 1951 version of *Show Boat*, they bought up the rights and prints to an earlier version so that the new one would have no competition.

Clifton Webb's real name was Webb Parmelee Hillenbeck.

The report after Fred Astaire's first screen test for M-G-M was: "Can't act, slightly bald, can dance a little."

The first song written into a film was "Mother, I Still Have You," written for *The Jazz Singer*, the first picture with sound.

Andy Devine, who later became a familiar figure in Westerns, worked as a human boom in the early days of sound films. He was so wide that he could hide a mike strapped to his chest or back, depending on which way he was facing.

The *Tarzan* call, developed by Johnny Weissmuller, who played the leading role in the series for a good number of years, was made electronically. It is based on a mountaineer's yodel that Weissmuller's father taught him when he was a boy, speeded up and played backwards three times the normal speed. The call was used in all the *Tarzan* pictures, even after Weissmuller left the series.

Winston Churchill once proposed marriage to actress Ethel Barrymore, but she turned him down.

Superstitious director Mervyn LeRoy always tried to get his lucky number, 62, into his pictures—as a house number, a license plate, etc. Anatole Litvak tried having at least one staircase with thirteen steps on the sets of his pictures. And William Wyler played a French lullaby on the fiddle before shooting a new picture.

The Creature from the Black Lagoon was filmed in 3-D. By wearing special glasses, you could see the film in three dimensions instead of two.

Olivia De Havilland and Joan Fontaine are sisters.

Joan Crawford won her film name in a contest run by *Photoplay* magazine, in which fans sent in names. Ms. Crawford's real name had been Lucille Le Sueur, and she was also known for a time as Billie Cassin. The winner received $1,000 and the actress her movie name.

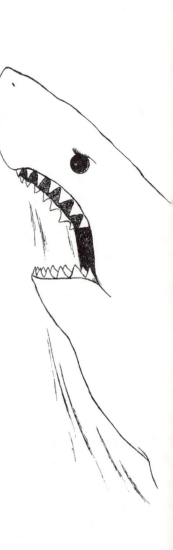

Shark experts Ron and Valerie Taylor were hired to film a twenty-five-foot great white shark for the movie *Jaws*, but could not find sharks that were longer than fifteen feet. To solve the problem, ex-jockey Carl Rizzo, four feet nine inches tall, was hired, given a specially made small diver's suit and small-scale equipment, and sent underwater in a small-scale shark cage. When a fifteen-foot great white was filmed next to the jockey and the cage, it appeared much larger.

For *Snow White and the Seven Dwarfs,* Walt Disney received one regular Academy Award and seven miniature ones.

Barbara Stanwyck's real name is Ruby Stevens.

At the time of her phenomenal success in *The Wizard of Oz,* Judy Garland was paid a salary of only $300 per week.

Actress Rita Hayworth married a Moslem prince, Aly Khan, in 1949.

Hollywood columnist Hedda Hopper had been a top leading lady in silent films.

Alan Ladd, who was not a particularly tall man, sometimes had to stand on a box in the filming of a scene with his leading lady.

The most expensive musical film ever made was *Hello, Dolly!,* which cost twenty million dollars.

34

Bing Crosby introduced more Oscar-winning songs in films than anyone else. They were: "Sweet Leilani" from *Waikiki Wedding*, "White Christmas" from *Holiday Inn*, "Swinging on a Star" from *Going My Way*, and "In the Cool, Cool, Cool of the Evening" from *Here Comes the Groom*.

The first actor to play *Tarzan* in the movies was Elmo Lincoln.

Catherine the Great of Russia has been the subject of more film biographies than anyone else. The second most popular subject is Abraham Lincoln, and third is Jack the Ripper.

Richard Burton has a long curved crease pressed into his pants to draw attention away from his bowed legs.

Marlon Brando's mother and Henry Fonda began acting with the Omaha Community Playhouse in the mid-1920s.

Shirley Temple's middle name is Jane.

Robert Mitchum once knocked out a champion boxer who happened to pick on a friend of his at a bar.

For his 1974 film *Young Frankenstein,* Mel Brooks bought the old sets and laboratory equipment from the Boris Karloff *Frankenstein* of 1931.

Lupe Velez, film star of the 1920s, had a Mexican Chihuahua that weighed just seven ounces and cost her seven hundred dollars a year to maintain.

Director Mervyn LeRoy's wife read *Gone With the Wind* and recommended that he secure the screen rights to the story, but LeRoy said there was no money in Civil War pictures and let it go.

Bruce Lee, born in San Francisco, returned to Hong Kong at the age of three months, and was a child film star from the ages of six to eighteen under the name of Lee Liu Loong, the Little Dragon. In 1958 he was shipped back to the United States because he was beginning to get into trouble as a street fighter in Hong Kong.

The first movie theaters were stores filled with a screen, a projector, and some folding chairs. Within a few years, there were thousands of theaters scattered across the country.

For one sequence in Alfred Hitchcock's *The Birds,* birds were strapped to the backs of children. When they ran out of the schoolhouse, the birds tried to fly away but couldn't, and began pecking at the kids, which was exactly what was required for the scene.

Lon Chaney, brought up by deaf-mute parents, said that this training helped him in his work as a silent film actor, because so much depended on his ability to get an idea across without sound.

Actor Stewart Granger's real name was James Stewart.

Robert Blake, known as TV's *Baretta,* started his film career in the *Our Gang* films of the 1930s. Another child role he played was that of the little boy in *The Treasure of Sierra Madre* who sold Humphrey Bogart the winning lottery ticket.

For one scene in *Way Down East,* a 1920 D. W. Griffith film, the action took place on a frozen river on which the ice was breaking up and rushing over a falls. In those days there were no doubles or stunt people, so leading lady Lillian Gish did the scene on a real ice floe, her long hair trailing into the frozen water, while leading man Richard Barthelmess jumped from floe to floe to reach her before she went over the falls. The rescue took place just in time, and Barthelmess had to jump from floe to floe back to safety with Ms. Gish in his arms.

Several years before starring as the bedeviled girl in *The Exorcist,* Linda Blair did a mustard commercial for TV.

The filming of *Gone With the Wind* was well underway before an actress was found to play Scarlett O'Hara, the female lead. A total of 149,000 feet of film, or twenty-four hours' worth, were used in screen tests, including some for Bette Davis, Susan Hayward, and Paulette Goddard. Finally, the producer's brother came on the set with Vivien Leigh, and she got the part immediately.

Rudolph Valentino's real name was Rodolfo Alfonzo Raffaelo Pierre Filibert Guglielmi di Valentina d'Antonguolla.

In 1930 the American film industry employed more people than Ford and General Motors put together.

Johnny Weissmuller, who played *Tarzan* for many years, was the 1924 Olympic swimming champion. He had been modeling bathing suits when a talent scout found him and offered him the role of *Tarzan*.

Actress Grace Kelly became Princess Grace when she married Prince Rainier of Monaco.

The Frankenstein monster's make-up, created by Universal Studios' make-up genius Jack Pierce, is copyrighted by Universal Studios. It cannot be copied for commercial purposes without their permission.

In the film *Camelot*, Vanessa Redgrave, as Guinevere, wears a gown completely covered by pumpkin seeds, which are stitched onto the fabric.

When Walter Wanger called Elizabeth Taylor in London to ask her to play the lead in *Cleopatra*, Ms. Taylor jokingly replied that she would do it for a million dollars. To her surprise, Wanger said yes, making her the highest paid actress the world has ever known.

Captain Blood starred Errol Flynn. *Son of Captain Blood* starred Errol's son, Sean Flynn.

It is a well-known fact that Samuel Goldwyn, the movie mogul who started out as poor boy Sammy Goldfish, was a master of malapropisms. Some of his more famous ones are:

"Include me out."

"A verbal contract isn't worth the paper it's written on."

"They're always biting the hand that lays the golden egg."

"In two words—Im possible."

"I want you to know that a Goldwyn comedy is not to be laughed at!"

And, concerning a fourteenth-century sun dial: "What will they think of next?"

Marlon Brando never learns lines for a film. His lines are written out for him and placed all over the set.

In the film *In Cold Blood*, the drawing of Humphrey Bogart in Perry Smith's jail cell was actually drawn by Robert Blake, who played Perry Smith.

Gary Cooper was once an artist for a local newspaper in his native Montana. Later, he turned to stunting for the movies, which paid him five dollars a fall.

For the initial showing of D. W. Griffith's *The Birth of a Nation,* a silent film, a seventy-piece orchestra was employed to play a special score.

The first Mickey Mouse cartoon, *Steamboat Willie,* appeared in 1928.

In 1912, when Lillian and Dorothy Gish, mere teen-agers, auditioned for D. W. Griffith, he chased them around the set with a pistol to test their reactions. They got the job.

W. C. Fields once earned money as a professional "drowner" at a concession stand in Atlantic City, New Jersey. He went out into the ocean, pretended he was drowning, and when he was being revived, a crowd would gather. The concession owner would sell hot dogs, ice cream, and drinks to the crowd and split the profits with Fields.

In the 1927 version of *Ben Hur*, the huge sea battle was re-enacted with a real boat. Many people were drowned jumping out of the boat. The later version of the story used miniatures to re-create the battle scenes.

Before Humphrey Bogart was offered the starring role in *High Sierra*, it was offered to George Raft. Raft turned it down because he didn't want to die in the end.

Cecil B. De Mille made his first film in a building that was half barn, half carriage wash.

Claudette Colbert, playing Poppaea in the 1932 production of *The Sign of the Cross*, had to take a milk bath in four hundred gallons of milk. That wasn't so bad, but the shooting took a week, and it was like bathing in smelly cheese after a few days.

Some of the first prints of *Frankenstein* were tinted green to add a ghastly glow to the already terrifying film.

William Boyd, who later became known as Hopalong Cassidy, was a terrible horseman when he started out in films. If he had any scenes on a horse, they had to be sure he was standing still. Later, as Hopalong, he studied riding seriously and became quite good at it.

For the shark thriller *Jaws*, three mechanical sharks were devised, all nicknamed by the crew "Bruce."

The stories of *Eloise*, the precocious child who lives at the Plaza Hotel, are based on Liza Minnelli as a child. They were written by her godmother, Kay Thompson, the actress.

Sophia Loren's real name is Sophia Scicolone.

The Roxy Theater in New York City was the largest theater built since the fall of Rome. The gigantic movie palace had its own hospital, six box offices, a radio studio, an apartment for Mr. Roxy, an orchestra of 110 musicians, five organists, and a corps of ushers who were reported to be ex-Marines.

Famous screen playwright Anita Loos began writing scripts for D. W. Griffith at the age of fourteen.

For the flood scene in *Noak's Ark*, a 1929 Warner Brothers production, an actual deluge of water was poured on stunt people and extras from overhead tanks, causing several casualties.

Broncho Billy Anderson, claiming to be an expert horseman for a part in the first film Western, *The Great Train Robbery*, mounted his horse on the wrong side and got thrown off. He tried three times before he stayed on the horse.

In a publicity stunt for *The Man I Killed*, a man who insisted he could survive such an ordeal was buried alive for twenty-four hours. During the night there was a terrific storm which washed away all traces of the burial place. A crew of thirty diggers worked half the night to locate him. The man demanded overtime pay.

The longest running movie is reported to be *Me Tarzan, You Jane*, which has been playing in an Egyptian movie theater since 1949.

Lon Chaney died in 1930 of throat cancer, leaving him in his last days to go back to his old practice of pantomime and sign language, which he used with his deaf-mute parents and in his silent films.

Billy Wilder is the only man in the history of the Academy Awards to have won Oscars in three different categories: writing, directing, and producing.

Laurence Olivier did the highest paid commercial in the history of TV for the Polaroid company for $1 million.

Nanook of the North, filmed in 1922 by Robert Flaherty, had no professional actors in it. All the players, even Nanook, were natives of the Far North.

Mel Blanc, the voice for Warner Brothers' cartoon character Bugs Bunny, was allergic to carrots. No substitute for carrots could be found that sounded like carrots on the sound track, so Blanc had to keep a bucket next to him, in which he could spit out the chewed carrots.

Tom Mix, famous cowboy star of early films, rode around Hollywood in a white limousine with a large pair of steer horns as a radiator ornament.

Early recording equipment was so sensitive that it picked up sounds made by certain fabrics. Therefore, taffeta could not be used at all, petticoats had to be made out of felt and wool rather than silk, and shoes had to be covered with felt and rubber.

In *Gone With the Wind*, for the scene where thousands of Confederate soldiers are lying dying and wounded at Atlanta station, it was originally planned to use dummies for all those bodies. However, the Screen Actors' Guild protested, and the studio had to hire all available extras to play the soldiers—about three thousand in all. Two thousand more bodies were still needed, so dummies were used in the farthest shots.

At one time, Jimmy Durante copyrighted his nose.

Erich von Stroheim appeared as an extra in *Birth of a Nation*.

48

From 1925 to 1930, 10,794 people were injured in film productions.

The Misfits, made in 1961, was the last film of both Clark Gable and Marilyn Monroe.

Shirley Temple was supposed to play the role of Dorothy in *The Wizard of Oz*, but Twentieth Century-Fox, who had her under contract, asked M-G-M for too much money. Thus, the part went to a newcomer, Judy Garland, giving her her big break.

The first werewolf movie, *The Werewolf*, was actually about a wolf-woman. It was made in 1913. *Werewolf of London* appeared in 1935, and *The Wolf Man* in 1941.

John Wayne's films have grossed more than three hundred million dollars at the box office, more than those of any other star in history.

The Great Train Robbery, the first real "Western," was filmed in the New Jersey.

Oliver Hardy played villains in films before he met Stan Laurel and formed the Laurel and Hardy comedy team.

Lana Turner's first name was made up for her by director Mervyn LeRoy. Her real name had been Julia Jean Mildred Frances Turner.

Gossip columnist Hedda Hopper's real name was Elda Furry.

Westerns filmed in Italy are called "spaghetti Westerns." Those shot in Israel have been labeled "bagel Westerns."

Humphrey Bogart spoke with a sort of lisp because his upper lip had been paralyzed from a splinter received during a shelling on his troopship in the Navy.

Greta Garbo claims that she has never received a love letter in her life.

Former stateswoman Clare Boothe Luce was once a child movie star for the Edison Company.

Dorothy Lamour was an elevator operator in a Chicago department store before she became a movie actress.

Beer cannot be faked in films; nothing else looks like beer except beer.

Once, Humphrey Bogart and a friend bought two stuffed pandas and took them to the El Morocco night club as their dates. A lady came by and touched one of the pandas and Bogart pushed her away, causing the woman to press charges of assault. The judge ruled that the panda was Mr. Bogart's personal property; therefore, he had a right to defend it.

Margaret Hamilton, who played the Wicked Witch of the West in *The Wizard of Oz,* was once a kindergarten teacher.

The earliest film record of a news event is the coronation of Czar Nicholas II in 1896, filmed by two Frenchmen.

Douglas Fairbanks had his friend Charlie Stevens, a grandson of Indian warrior Geronimo, appear in many of his films. In *The Black Pirate,* made in 1926, Stevens played many roles; he would be blown up in one scene and reappear in another.

The immortal Babe Ruth of baseball fame appeared as himself in the Lou Gehrig story, *Pride of the Yankees.*

Charlie Chaplin's leading lady for eight years had been Edna Purviance. Chaplin made sure she received a weekly check from his studio until she died, in 1958.

Tarzan star Johnny Weissmuller was the one who chose Johnny Sheffield to play the part of his son, Boy, even though Sheffield confided to Weissmuller that he couldn't swim. After the contract was signed, Weissmuller secretly taught the boy to swim.

The first thing to be photographed in motion was a racehorse, in 1872, to settle a dispute about whether all four of the horse's hoofs were ever off the ground at the same time. It was accomplished by setting up a row of cameras along a track and setting them off in rapid succession as the horse raced by. The results, when projected, showed that indeed the four feet did come off the ground at the same time.

The premiere of the film *Underwater*, starring Jane Russell, was held under water. Members of the audience were equipped with air tanks or aqualungs, and watched the film on an undersea screen.

John Lindsay, former mayor of New York City, had a small role as a senator in Otto Preminger's movie *The Terrorists*.

The membership of the Stunt Men's Association of Motion Pictures was eighty-nine in 1963, and thirty-four of them were used in the film *It's a Mad, Mad, Mad, Mad World*.

Georges Méliès, known as the father of trick photography, became interested in film trickery by accident. He was filming the Place de l'Opéra in Paris one day while a bus was going by. The camera jammed, Méliès unjammed it and continued filming. By then, the bus had gone and a hearse was passing by. When he developed the film the bus seemed to have turned into a hearse right before his eyes.

Mickey Mouse has been awarded more honors and prizes, including an Academy Award, than any other character in history.

Stan Laurel was Charlie Chaplin's understudy on the stage in England, before they came to Hollywood.

The granddaddy of all monster films was *The Lost World,* produced in 1925, which was the first monster film to use prehistoric beasts and special effects trickery.

The only performers ever to have won three Oscars for acting were Katharine Hepburn for *Morning Glory* (1932), *Guess Who's Coming to Dinner* (1967), and *The Lion in Winter* (1968); Walter Brennan for *Come and Get It* (1936), *Kentucky* (1938), and *The Westerner* (1940); and Ingrid Bergman for *Gaslight* (1944), *Anastasia* (1956), and *Murder on the Orient Express* (1974).

June Allyson was once understudy to Betty Hutton.

The name "Buster" was given to Buster Keaton by a then unknown traveling illusionist named Harry Houdini.

Musical film star June Haver abandoned her Hollywood career in 1953 to become a nun. However, she later left the convent and married actor Fred MacMurray.

When his famous horse Trigger died, Roy Rogers had him stuffed. He said he just couldn't bear to part with him.

Until he learned about sports from a swimming pool instructor, Johnny Weissmuller had aspired to grow up and become part of Al Capone's gang in Chicago.

Mae West wrote most of her own dialogue for her films.

Robert Mitchum got his start in a Hopalong Cassidy film.

Sonja Henie, Norway's Olympic figure-skating champion, accumulated a forty-seven million dollar fortune as a Hollywood film star, making her the wealthiest skater the world has known.

After the Wall Street crash in 1929, when movie Studios realized that cheap entertainment during hard times would be a lucrative business, Warner Brothers put Joan Blondell in thirty-two pictures in twenty-seven months.

M-G-M created a gigantic swimming pool on the M-G-M lot for its money-making aquatic star, Esther Williams.

Robert Blake's real name is Michael Gubitosi.

Harry Carey, considered by some experts to be the greatest cowboy in films, learned to ride a horse from the mounted policemen in New York City.

Judy Garland's funeral in New York in 1969 brought out twenty-two thousand fans to pay their last respects, the greatest tribute to a past film star since the death of Valentino in 1926.

Katharine Hepburn married Ludlow Ogden Smith in 1928. She insisted he change his surname to Ogden so that she would not be known as the second Kate Smith.

Liza Minnelli, daughter of Judy Garland, who played Dorothy in *The Wizard of Oz*, married Jack Haley, Jr., son of Jack Haley, who played The Tin Man in the same film.

During the filming of *The Wizard of Oz*, Margaret Hamilton, playing the part of the Wicked Witch of the West, was badly burned. She was made to "appear" and "disappear" by means of a trap door, right next to another trap door through which smoke and flame were sent up just before she came up through her trap door. The timing was just a little off, and the flames did not disappear completely before Ms. Hamilton came up, and the fire melted the green copper-based paint that covered her face, giving her third-degree burns. She was out recuperating for three months.

Shirley Temple earned over a million dollars as a film star before she was ten years old.

Cyprus has more movie theaters per total population than any other country in the world.

Spencer Tracy received more Academy Award nominations—nine—than any other male star.

Bela Lugosi was asked to play the Frankenstein monster before Boris Karloff, but he refused because it wasn't a speaking part.

Showman Mike Todd, who produced *Around the World in 80 Days,* was once stopped by a flock of sheep on his way to Colorado. He bought the animals, figuring he could use them in his next film.

The make-up for the cast of *The Planet of the Apes* took as long as five hours to apply. At mealtimes, the actors had to use mirrors at first to find their mouths, and drinking, of course, had to be done through straws.

The first in-flight movie was shown in an airplane in 1929.

The first all-talking picture was Warner Brothers' *Lights of New York*. *The Jazz Singer* had come out before, with sound, but had only three songs and brief dialogue—the rest was silent.

In 1961, it was calculated that at a single sitting, movie theaters around the world could seat 56,745,451 people.

A fan magazine in 1932 published Tom Mix's often-exaggerated medical history, listing (and showing on a skeleton) his twenty-six injuries.

In the original *Ten Commandments*, made in 1923, the opening and closing of the Red Sea were created by Roy Pomeroy, the special-effects wizard, who filmed Jell-O with water running over it. It was so realistic that Pomeroy had to prove to the Society for the Prevention of Cruelty to Animals that what appeared to be horses swallowed up by the ocean on the screen was really double exposures and Jell-O.

During the shooting of *Casablanca,* starring Humphrey Bogart and Ingrid Bergman, nobody, even the director, knew how the picture was going to end until the last scene was ready to be shot. The writers kept working on it all the way through.

A bill was once introduced in Congress to prohibit the shipment to other countries of American films in which ex-convicts, bandits, or outlaws appeared. The bill was defeated.

The masterpiece of Hollywood make-up was Lon Chaney's Quasimodo in *The Hunchback of Notre Dame.* It took him 4½ hours each day to get into costume, which consisted of a seventy-pound hump and harness, plus football shoulder and leg pads and a breastplate. Once strapped in, he could not stand up straight. Chaney did all his own make-up, which in this case included a distorted face made with mortician's wax.

During the filming of the picture *Wings,* which won the first Academy Award in 1928, Gary Cooper asked to do a scene over again, because he had picked his nose right in the middle of it. The director, William A. Wellman, advised Cooper to go on picking his nose, because that scene had turned out beautifully.

The first movie capital of the world was not Hollywood but Fort Lee, New Jersey. The East Coast later lost out to the West Coast because California weather was better for all-year-round filming.

Paul Newman believes pictures beginning with the letter "H" are lucky for him, based on his experiences with *Hud, The Hustler,* and *Hombre.* When he was asked to do the Lew Archer detective movie, he agreed if they changed the private eye's name to *Harper,* which they did.

Robert Flaherty's first version of *Nanook of the North* was completely destroyed by fire. Flaherty took it in his stride, and promptly returned to the frozen lands of the Arctic to reshoot the entire picture.

Before becoming a movie cowboy, Tom Mix had been a sheriff in Kansas and Oklahoma, a deputy U.S. marshal, and a Texas Ranger.

The costume of Frankenstein's monster in *Bride of Frankenstein* threw Boris Karloff off balance. He wrenched his hip and spent most of the time filming in bandages.

Cary Grant's real name is Archibald Alexander Leach.

Carmen Miranda, the "Brazilian Bombshell," who sang and danced Latin rhythms with fruit piled high on her head, was imported to help open up a Latin-American film market during World War II when the European market was closed.

Doris Day had originally wanted to be a dancer, but at age fifteen she broke her leg and turned to singing instead.

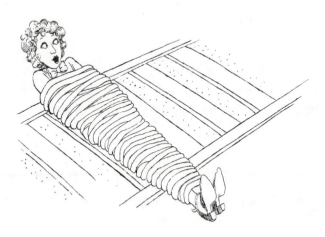

The first American movie serial was *The Perils of Pauline*, starring Pearl White, an accomplished acrobat as well as an actress, who did all her own stunts.

Fred Astaire was such a perfectionist that he did one number for *Holiday Inn* thirty-eight times before being satisfied with it. When he started on the picture he had weighed 140 pounds. At the end of the filming, he was down to 126.

The people of Taiwan are the champion movie-goers of all time. The average person there goes to the movies sixty-six times a year.

In the early days of sound movies, sound was such a startling new thing that movie critics couldn't get over it. One reviewer, on *Don Juan,* said: "It is an interesting fact that the swishing of the swords can be heard with startling clarity throughout the action of the duel, and as soon as the duel is over, the swishing stops. Not one swish too many."

Donald Duck made his film debut in an animated cartoon called *The Wise Little Hen,* in 1934.

Jimmy Durante had his nose insured for $100,000 by Lloyd's of London.

The Wizard of Oz cost $3,200,000 to produce.

For thirty years following the bombing of Pearl Harbor in 1941, Bob Hope has traveled all over the world to entertain servicemen.

Eddie Egan, the real-life "narc" on whose exploits *The French Connection* is based, appeared in the film as Gene Hackman's superior.

Judy Garland's real name was Frances Gumm.

Only thirty minutes of the entire 222 minutes of *Gone With the Wind* are without music.

Cary Grant was the first important movie star to go free-lance. From the time his Paramount contract ended in 1936, he never again signed with any studio exclusively.

Rita Hayworth was in twenty-four films before she decided to lose weight, raise her hairline through electrolysis, and change her hair color to copper red. The impact of her new look led to major film roles, and then stardom.

Boris Karloff turned down the role of *The Invisible Man* because he didn't want to remain unseen until the end of the picture. Claude Rains got the part, which launched his career.

W. C. Fields once spiked Baby LeRoy's baby bottle with liquor, because the youngster was stealing so many scenes. The rest of the day's shooting was called off when Baby LeRoy showed definite signs of being drunk.

Actress Kay Francis left a fortune of two million dollars for the training of guide dogs for the blind.

Before copyright laws protected films, producers used to insert bold trademarks into key scenes of a movie so that film pirates would have a hard time stealing their films.

In *The Day of the Locust,* Dick Powell at a premiere in Hollywood is played by his son and look-alike, Dick Powell, Jr.

Jaws grossed over forty-one million dollars as of March 1976, making it the biggest money-making film of all time. The cost to make the picture was approximately eight million dollars.

In the scene in *Gone With the Wind* in which the city of Atlanta burns, old movie sets from *The Last of the Mohicans, King Kong, The Garden of Allah,* and *Little Lord Fauntleroy* were set on fire.

After *Summer Stock* shooting was completed, it was decided to go back and add one more musical number. Judy Garland, meanwhile, had lost a great deal of weight from a diet. Thus, in the "Get Happy" number, the one that was added on, she appears considerably smaller than in the rest of the film.

One of the loudest screen kisses is recorded for Jack Palance while kissing Shelley Winters in *I Died a Thousand Times.*

For the filming of *King Kong*, several models of the giant gorilla were constructed. There were six miniatures, about eighteen inches high, a huge head and shoulders, and huge hands for close-ups. The flesh was made of rubber and covered with rabbit fur. A mechanical hand and arm eight feet long were constructed, and inside the furry arm was a contraption that could raise and lower it. It even had a mechanism to open and close the fingers.

Stan Laurel, before he came to Hollywood and teamed up with Oliver Hardy, was called Stan Jefferson. He changed his name when he realized it had thirteen letters in it.

Burt Lancaster started out as a circus performer. For most of his action work in movies, he does his own stunt work, because of his acrobatic experience.

Warren Beatty and Shirley MacLaine are brother and sister.

Lon Chaney, Sr., once wrote an entry for make-up for the *Encyclopaedia Britannica*.

Jerry Lewis' real name is Joseph Levitch.

In 1940, five out of fifteen of the highest salaries in the United States went to movie people.

Harold Russell, a veteran of World War II who lost both his hands in an explosion in the war, played the role of a handless veteran in *The Best Years of Our Lives* because he thought it might help others similarly handicapped. Russell received the Oscar for best supporting actor for his role.

Singer Marni Nixon, a former M-G-M messenger, has sung for many of Hollywood's top stars: Margaret O'Brien in *The Big Sleep;* Deborah Kerr in *The King and I* and *An Affair to Remember;* Natalie Wood in *West Side Story;* and Audrey Hepburn in *My Fair Lady*. She has only appeared on screen once, as a nun in *The Sound of Music*.

The first screen vampire appeared in 1896, in Georges Méliès' short film *The Devil's Castle*, thirty-five years before Universal's famous Dracula appeared with Bela Lugosi. However, Lugosi played the first film vampire that *talked*.

71

In 1927, silent film comedian Harold Lloyd was the highest paid of all film stars; his weekly income was between $30,000 and $40,000. In 1920, a bomb "prop" had gone off, blowing off his thumb and forefinger, but Lloyd went on making films and doing his own stunts, wearing a rubber glove on the fingerless hand.

The film *Madame Butterfly* was banned in Japan because during an embrace between Sylvia Sidney and her American hero, Ms. Sidney's elbow shows, which was tantamount to nudity in Japan.

Hughie Mack, an early film comedian, got his start when he fell asleep on a job as an extra. The director, impressed by his snoring, woke him up to sign a contract.

Actor Audie Murphy was America's most decorated soldier when he arrived in Hollywood. One role he played in movies was that of himself, in the movie *To Hell and Back*, about his own war experiences.

Edward G. Robinson's real name was Emanuel Goldenberg.

Before color movies, most costumes were made in black, white, gray, or red. (Red photographs blacker than black.)

Mickey Rooney, the perpetual boy-next-door type from the Andy Hardy films, has been married seven times, once to Ava Gardner.

Actor Tony Randall said that he saw his file kept by the CIA and it read: "We have nothing on this man but he has been for peace."

For the roles of the Munchkins in *The Wizard of Oz,* all the midgets that could be found were employed, but there weren't enough, so children were hired. However, midgets got the lead parts, with children playing lesser roles farther away from the camera and microphones.

Snow White and the Seven Dwarfs, produced by Walt Disney in 1937, was the first full-length animated feature put out by the Disney Studios.

Ginger Rogers' real name is Virginia Katherine McMath.

While making the film *Bonnie Prince Charlie*, David Niven was in a battle scene where he tripped, accidentally thrusting his sword deep into the leg of the man in front of him. After the blade was pulled out the man started limping away and the stunned Niven called to him about having a doctor look at his leg. The man rolled up his trouser leg to reveal that his leg was not hurt —the original had been lost in a *real* battle somewhere.

Deanna Durbin tried out for the voice of Snow White when she was still an unknown, and Disney rejected her because she sounded "too old" for the part. Later, at Universal Studios, she saved the movie company from bankruptcy and became one of Hollywood's most popular stars.

The Keystone Kops were invented as the result of an experiment by Mack Sennett and his girl friend, actress Mabel Normand. Normand went into a Shriners' parade, holding a doll wrapped in a blanket, and began accusing a total stranger of being the father of her child. The police came, a crowd gathered, and pandemonium broke out. All the action was filmed. After studying the results, Sennett got the idea for the Keystone Kops.

For close-ups in *Dracula,* flashlights were shone into Bela Lugosi's eyes, which meant he had to remain perfectly still or the lights would show up on his nose or forehead.

The film version of *Dracula* was prepared for Lon Chaney, but Chaney died and the role was offered to Bela Lugosi, who had played the role on the Broadway stage.

Sam Warner, who was responsible for the first sound film, *The Jazz Singer,* died twenty-four hours before the film's premiere, so he never knew how it changed film history.

It took an entire day of shooting to film half a minute showing King Kong moving. Each step Kong took required a dozen exposures.

Robert Mitchum once served seven days on a Georgia chain gang.

Western stars were often closely associated with their horses. Some famous pairs were William S. Hart and Fritz; Gene Autry and Champion; Roy Rogers and Trigger; Hopalong Cassidy and Topper; Tom Mix and Tony; The Cisco Kid and Diablo; Dale Evans and Buttermilk.

Boris Karloff, Lon Chaney, Jr., and Bela Lugosi all played the *Frankenstein* monster at one time or another.

Greta Garbo once had a job in Sweden lathering men's faces in a Stockholm barber shop.

Although *Snow White and the Seven Dwarfs* was released in 1937, Disney Studio artists were at work exploring the characters in the story as early as 1934. An early list of possible names for the dwarfs included:

Scrappy	Doleful	Crabby
Hoppy	Awful	Daffy
Dirty	Gabby	Puffy
Dumpy	Flabby	Chesty
Hungry	Snoopy	Busy
Thrifty	Shifty	Biggy
Weepy	Helpful	Gaspy

In 1934, M-G-M loaned out their star Clark Gable to Columbia Pictures as a kind of "punishment" to Gable for making too many salary demands. At Columbia, Gable made *It Happened One Night* with Claudette Colbert, won the Oscar, the film was voted Best Picture of 1934, and it was the first picture in history to make a clean sweep of the Academy honors.

Humphrey Bogart, aware that a private detective had been following him, called up the fellow's agency and said, "This is Humphrey Bogart. You got a man on my tail. Would you check with him and find out where I am?"

Fay Wray became famous for her remarkable scream in the picture *King Kong*. When the picture was finished, Ms. Wray screamed in the sound room for an extra five minutes so that technicians could splice in more of her screams wherever they deemed it necessary.

Jerry Lewis' house, in a fashionable suburb outside of Hollywood, has a notice posted outside reading that it is open to Sunshine, Children and God.

Irving Thalberg was head of M-G-M before he was thirty years old; Darryl F. Zanuck was head producer at Warner Brothers at twenty-six; David O. Selznick was vice president in charge of production at RKO at age twenty-nine; Matthew Fox was assistant to the president of Universal Studios at twenty-nine; Pandro Berman took over RKO before he was thirty-two; Garson Kanin at twenty-six directed top movies; Hal B. Wallis was an executive producer at Warner Brothers at thirty-two.

For the picture *Airport,* the entire interior of a 707 jet plane was constructed on a sound stage.

Rin-Tin-Tin, the famous movie dog, played a dog suspected of being a wolf in *The Clash of the Wolves.* As part of the plot, he was "disguised" with a fake beard, and when the beard fell off, the townspeople recognized him immediately.

79

There was some doubt in Paramount executives' collective minds that Marlon Brando was right for the part of The Godfather because he wasn't old enough, and some wanted him screen-tested for the part. Brando agreed to a trial run, and a video tape machine was brought to his home. On the spot, Brando created the character of Don Corleone, using tissue paper in his cheeks to give him jowls and black shoe polish around his eyes to age him properly.

Richard Burton's real name is Richard Jenkins.

As a result of the film *Intolerance* by D. W. Griffith, Griffith was invited to take charge of the entire Russian film industry. He declined the offer.

Red Buttons' real name is Aaron Schwatt.

Robert Stack, later known for his role as Elliott Ness in TV's series "The Untouchables" first appeared on the movie screen in *First Love*, the film in which young Deanna Durbin, Universal's top star, received her first screen kiss.

There was once an ordinance passed specifying the number of sheep that could be herded through the intersection in Los Angeles which is now known as Hollywood and Vine.

When *The Silver Chalice* was first shown on TV, Paul Newman, embarrassed about his performance in his first film, took an ad in a local paper asking people not to watch it.

During the shooting of the film *Peck's Bad Boy,* young Jackie Cooper was having a rare hard time making the tears come for a crying scene. He was too smart to fall for the usual tricks about being told his dog had died, but when the producer took Jackie's state of mind out on the director and shouted that he was fired, Jackie burst into tears. Of course, this was another trick; the producer knew that the director was Jackie's friend.

William S. Hart, the first star of "adult" Westerns, grew up in Minnesota and Wisconsin, where there were still Blackfeet and Sioux Indians who had fought Custer in the Indian wars. Hart could speak Sioux at the age of six.

Silent screen star Mae Murray paid for her jewelry with bags of gold dust.

During the showing of *Psycho,* no one was admitted to the theater after the show started.

Doris Day's real name is Doris von Kappelhoff.

Fourteen years of unemployment after the end of the *Our Gang* series, Spanky McFarland placed an ad in a local trade journal: "Childhood (3–16) spent as leader of *Our Gang* comedies. Won't someone give me the opportunity to make a living in the business I love and know so well? Have beanie, will travel."

Three of Hollywood's biggest movie moguls started out as: a furrier (Adolph Zukor), a scrap-metal dealer (Louis B. Mayer), and a glove manufacturer (Samuel Goldwyn).

Walter Wanger made the picture *Riot in Cell Block 11* as a direct result of a jail term he himself had served.

James Garner's real name is James Baumgarner.

Movie stars who died before the age of forty include Jean Harlow (26), Kay Kendall (33), Marilyn Monroe (36), Mario Lanza (38), Carole Lombard (34), Rudolph Valentino (30), Sabu (39), James Dean (24), Robert Walker (32), Marta Toren (27), Brandon de Wilde (30), John Garfield (39), Carole Landis (29), Jayne Mansfield (34), Carmen Miranda (38), Maria Montez (32), and Sal Mineo (37).

When the first silent films were shown, the action on the screen was so overwhelming to audiences who had never seen anything like it before that the first few rows of the audience often rose and fled in panic. This was particularly true of the showing of an oncoming train.

Win Min Than, a Burmese girl, came to the United States to promote the film *The Purple Plain,* in which she starred with Gregory Peck. While here, she was offered parts as a Hawaiian hula dancer, an American Indian, an Arab half-caste, a Chinese slave, and an Okinawan girl. She decided to go back to Burma and be a housewife.

During the filming of *The Sting*, a Universal Studios tour bus came through the lot while Paul Newman and Robert Redford were playing a scene. Overeager tourists jumped out of the bus and ran up to the actors, breathlessly asking for autographs. Today, because of that incident, none of the tour buses are opened where scenes are being filmed.

Before 1955, the life-span of a film was shorter than a successful Broadway play, roughly one to two years. Within eighteen months, most films were back in vaults. Then Hollywood began releasing its films to TV, proving that movies had a life after their first run.

Twentieth Century-Fox had a policy of featuring blond female stars in their top films, starting with Shirley Temple on through Alice Faye, Betty Grable, June Haver, Sonja Henie, and others.

In one of her films, Olivia de Havilland rode a horse which later became famous as "Trigger," when Roy Rogers bought him.

When Nazism was rising in Germany, Fritz Lang, the director, was still working in films there. Goebbels, one of Hitler's major henchmen, called Mr. Lang to his office and asked him to take over the German film industry. "Wonderful, wonderful," was Lang's reply, but that evening, with only what he could wear or carry in his pockets, he left Germany.

Roy Rogers' real name is Leonard Slye.

Thirty thousand square feet (Warner Brothers soundstages 11 and 4) were used to create a replica of the Washington *Post* newsroom which is depicted in *All the President's Men*, a true story of two Washington *Post* reporters.

John Wayne's son Michael produced the movie *McLintock* in 1963.

Three performers have won Oscars for mute roles: John Mills for his nonspeaking role in *Ryan's Daughter;* Jane Wyman for her role as a deaf mute in *Johnny Belinda;* and Patty Duke for her role as the blind and deaf Helen Keller in *The Miracle Worker*.

Stan Laurel and Charlie Chaplin shared a room in a boardinghouse when they first came to the United States. Cooking was not allowed in the room, so Chaplin played the violin or the cello while Stan fried food on a forbidden hot plate.

Dalton Trumbo was the highest paid screen writer in Hollywood when he was subpoenaed to appear before the House Committee on Un-American Activities and became black-listed. In 1956 the Oscar for the Best Motion Picture Story was awarded to Robert Rich. When no one rose to collect the trophy, Jesse Lasky, Jr., vice president of the Screen Writers Guild, accepted it on behalf of his "good friend." Later, it turned out there was no such person as screen writer Robert Rich . . . that was a false name used by Trumbo, who would not have been able to get a job in Hollywood under his real name. The embarrassment helped to do away with the Hollywood black list, which had ended many a career, based on alleged affiliations with feared political groups.

The first child star awarded an Oscar was Jackie Cooper as best actor in the picture *Skippy*.

Claudette Colbert, winner of the 1934 Best Actress award for her role in *It Happened One Night*, did not expect to win, and was boarding a train for New York at the time of the announcement. She was whisked away to the presentation theater, made a quick acceptance while the other awards were interrupted, and was hustled back to her train.

At the 1933 Academy Awards, Will Rogers, the master of ceremonies, asked "best actress" nominees May Robson and Diana Wynyard up to the speakers' table, and everyone assumed it was to present them with a tie award. However, Rogers gave them each a kiss and then announced that the award had gone to Katharine Hepburn for her role in *Morning Glory*.

In the same year, as Rogers was getting ready to hand out the best director award, he said "Come and get it, Frank," (meaning Frank Lloyd, for *Lady for a Day*) and the wrong Frank (Capra) started up the aisle. Capra said, after discovering his error, that his return to his seat was "the longest crawl in history."

The Oscar is said to have been named after the uncle of Margaret Herrick, a retired director of the Academy of Motion Picture Arts and Sciences, in 1931.

Luise Rainer became the first player, male or female, to repeat as an Oscar winner, and was the first actress to win it in two consecutive years.

Following are the names of famous movie personalities and their famous offspring.

Offspring	Parents
Candice Bergen	Edgar Bergen
Jeff Bridges Beau Bridges	Lloyd Bridges
Alan Alda	Robert Alda
Susan Strasberg	Lee Strasberg
Michael Douglas	Kirk Douglas
Kris Tabori	Viveca Lindfors
Jane Fonda Peter Fonda	Henry Fonda
Jack Haley, Jr.	Jack Haley
Luci Arnaz Desi Arnaz, Jr.	Lucille Ball and Desi Arnaz
Liza Minnelli	Judy Garland and Vincente Minnelli
Lynn Redgrave Vanessa Redgrave	Sir Michael Redgrave
Mia Farrow	Maureen O'Sullivan and John Farrow
David Carradine	John Carradine

Marlo Thomas	Danny Thomas
Ricky Nelson	Ozzie and Harriet Nelson
David Ladd Alan Ladd, Jr.	Alan Ladd
Hayley Mills	John Mills
Jim Mitchum	Robert Mitchum
Geraldine Chaplin	Charlie Chaplin
Broderick Crawford	Helen Broderick
June Lockhart	Gene Lockhart
Tatum O'Neal	Ryan O'Neal
Keenan Wynn	Ed Wynn
Lon Chaney, Jr.	Lon Chaney
Nancy Sinatra	Frank Sinatra
Bonnie Raitt	John Raitt
Noah Beery, Jr.	Noah Beery
John Barrymore, Jr.	John Barrymore
Douglas Fairbanks, Jr.	Douglas Fairbanks

Joan Fontaine and Olivia de Havilland, sisters in real life, were both Academy Award candidates for the 1941 Best Actress award. Fontaine won for her part in *Suspicion*.

Ten-year-old Tatum O'Neal was the youngest performer ever to win an Academy Award, for best supporting actress in *Paper Moon*, 1973. She wore a tuxedo to the presentations.

For the four war years starting in 1943, the Oscar was made out of plaster, because metal was an essential war material.

At the 1950 Academy Awards ceremonies, *All About Eve* received fourteen nominations—an Academy record.

While shooting the dance number "Cheek to Cheek" in the film *Top Hat* with Ginger Rogers and Fred Astaire, Ms. Rogers' feathered gown began to molt, and feathers came down on the set like a snowstorm. The feathers were swept off the set and new ones glued on again, but the next time they danced, feathers flew again. More sweeping and gluing. This happened many times before the feathers stayed securely in place. In the final shooting, an occasional feather was still flying, but astute cameramen tried hard to avoid filming them.

The dual roles of Dr. Jekyll and Mr. Hyde have been played in American films by King Baggott, John Barrymore, Fredric March, and Spencer Tracy.

When Louis B. Mayer saw Ava Gardner's screen test, he is reported to have said, "She can't talk, she can't act, she's terrific."

After the Marx Brothers had waited several hours outside Irving Thalberg's office at M-G-M for an appointment made in advance, they emptied the contents of the secretary's wastebasket on the floor and set it on fire. Thalberg finally came out.

The book or play most often made into a movie has been Victor Hugo's *Les Miserables*. There are thirteen or fourteen film versions of the story.

Rondo Hatton's awesome features, caused by illness, got him a part as a Neanderthal-type monster in *House of Horrors*.

Fred MacMurray was once a saxophone player.

One biographer of Bruce Lee reported that he had the sweat glands removed from under his armpits so that he would look better.

Ava Gardner got her start in films because her brother-in-law, a professional photographer, took pictures of her and displayed them in a Fifth Avenue store window in New York. An M-G-M employee happened to see them and passed on the word, which led to a screen test.

Cheetah in the Tarzan series is actually a number of chimpanzees. Some are used for close-ups and some for running and swinging on the vines.

Peter Benchley, author of the book *Jaws*, appeared in the film as a reporter.

BARBARA SEULING, a native New Yorker, studied art and literature at Columbia University. She has spent most of her time since as a free-lance illustrator, editor, and writer, except for working one summer at the World's Fair in 1964, where her office was directly over a nuclear fission display, accompanied by a loud "boom!" precisely every four minutes.

The author of *The Last Legal Spitball and Other Little-Known Facts About Sports* and *You Can't Eat Peanuts in Church and Other Little-Known Laws*, Barbara lives in Manhattan.